This book belongs to:

____

Made in the USA
Las Vegas, NV
10 October 2021

32056489R00065